G

CENGAGE Learning

GW00649696

Novels for Students, Volume 27

Project Editor: Ira Mark Milne Rights Acquisition and Management: Vernon English, Leitha Etheridge-Sims, Aja Perales, Sue Rudolph Composition: Evi Abou-El-Seoud Manufacturing: Drew Kalasky

Imaging: Lezlie Light

Product Design: Pamela A. E. Galbreath, Jennifer Wahi Content Conversion: Civie Green, Katrina Coach Product Manager: Meggin Condino © 2008 Gale, Cengage Learning

For product information and technology assistance, contact us at **Gale Customer Support, 1-800-877-4253.**

For permission to use material from this text or product, submit all requests online at **www.cengage.com/permissions.**

Further permissions questions can be emailed to **permissionrequest@cengage.com** While every effort has been made to ensure the reliability of the information presented in this publication, Gale, a part of Cengage Learning, does not guarantee the accuracy of the data contained herein. Gale accepts no payment for listing; and inclusion in the publication of any organization, agency, institution, publication, service, or individual does not imply endorsement of the editors or publisher. Errors brought to the attention of the publisher and verified to the satisfaction of the publisher will be corrected in future editions.

Gale
27500 Drake Rd.
Farmington Hills, MI, 48331-3535

ISBN-13: 978-0-7876-8684-0
ISBN-10: 0-7876-8684-0
ISSN 1094-3552

This title is also available as an e-book.

ISBN-13: 978-1-4144-3831-3
ISBN-10: 1-4144-3831-1
Contact your Gale, a part of Cengage Learning sales
representative for ordering information.

Printed in the United States of America
1 2 3 4 5 6 7 12 11 10 09 08

The Talented Mr. Ripley

Patricia Highsmith 1955

Introduction

The Talented Mr. Ripley is the first of five books in the Ripley series by Patricia Highsmith, an American writer who moved permanently to Europe in 1963. The series features her best-known character, Tom Ripley. Highsmith's suspense novel *The Talented Mr. Ripley* was first published in 1955 and was republished in 1999 by Vintage. The edition is out of print but second-hand copies are available. The book was also published in 1999 by Everyman in an anthology consisting of three of the Ripley novels, titled *The Talented Mr. Ripley, Ripley Under Ground, Ripley's Game.* As of June

2007, this book is still available.

The novel's themes include the nature of identity, the relationship of the real to the imagined, and homosexuality. Ripley literally gets away with murder and the innocent characters suffer in an amoral world that disconcerts the reader by subverting expectations. The novel exemplifies Highsmith's rejection of the honest, straight-talking hero of conventional crime fiction in favor of the morally compromised or criminal protagonist. The atmosphere of menace that Highsmith creates, with the relatively low level of actual violence, justify the English novelist Graham Greene's characterization of her in his Foreword to her short story collection *Eleven* as "the poet of apprehension rather than fear."

Author Biography

Patricia Highsmith was born Mary Patricia Plangman in Fort Worth, Texas, on January 19, 1921, the only child of Jay Bernard Plangman, a graphic artist, and Mary Coates Highsmith, an illustrator and fashion designer. Highsmith's parents separated before she was born, and she was raised by her grandparents. At six years of age, Highsmith went to live with her mother and stepfather, Stanley Highsmith, in Greenwich Village, New York. She had an unhappy childhood and was not close to her mother. Highsmith was later to discover that when her mother was pregnant with her, she tried to abort the fetus by drinking turpentine.

The young Highsmith showed talent in painting and sculpting, but she made up her mind to be a writer. She attended Julia Richman High School, New York City, where she edited the school newspaper and read books by writers such as Leo Tolstoy, Fyodor Dostoyevsky, and Charles Dickens. She was particularly intrigued by Karl Menninger's book, *The Human Mind* (1930), which featured case studies of kleptomaniacs, pyromaniacs, and serial killers, because she realized that seemingly normal people could be hiding extreme mental pathology. Highsmith continued her education at Barnard College, University of Columbia, where she studied English, Latin, and Greek, and published short stories in the *Barnard Quarterly*.

After graduating in 1942, Highsmith lived in Manhattan and earned a living by writing text for comic strips. In 1944, she was admitted to Yaddo, the artists' colony in Saratoga Springs, New York, based on recommendations by the writer Truman Capote and others. While at Yaddo she got engaged to a fellow writer, Marc Brandel, but broke off the engagement shortly before the wedding, ostensibly because of her fear of being a mother.

Highsmith published her first novel, *Strangers on a Train*, a suspense thriller about a psychopath who commits what he hopes is the perfect murder, in 1950. The film director Alfred Hitchcock purchased the movie and stage rights for 6,800 dollars. The film was released in 1951. It proved a great success and Highsmith became famous overnight.

Highsmith's second novel, *The Price of Salt*, appeared in 1952 under the pseudonym Claire Morgan (other names under which Highsmith published are Mary Patricia Highsmith, Patricia Plangman, and Mary Patricia Plangman). The book was remarkable for its time in that it portrayed a lesbian relationship that ended happily. Highsmith admitted that she had fallen in love with the woman who had served as the model for the love object character in the novel, though she never publicly acknowledged her lesbianism. Highsmith went on to publish another novel about the quest for the perfect murder, *The Blunderer* (1954), which she followed in 1955 with *The Talented Mr. Ripley.* Highsmith wrote of the completed novel in her nonfiction work *Plotting and Writing Suspense Fiction* (1966), "No book was easier for me to write, and I often had the feeling Ripley was writing it and I was merely typing." The novel was given a special award by the Mystery Writers of America in 1956 and in 1957, it was awarded the Grand Prix de Littérature Policière and the Edgar Allan Poe Scroll of the Mystery Writers of America.

Highsmith's novel *The Two Faces of January* (1964) was awarded the Silver Dagger Award for best crime novel of the year by the Crime Writers Association of England in 1964. Other major novels include *People Who Knock on the Door* (1983), and *Found in the Street* (1986). In her later novels, Highsmith began to address social issues. *A Dog's Ransom*(1972) comments on the ineffectualness of law enforcement agencies, while *Edith's Diary* (1977) explores the ways in which society forces women into subservient roles.

Highsmith also published short story collections. *Little Tales of Misogyny* (1974) contributed to the common criticism that she portrayed women negatively. In *The Animal-Lover's Book of Beastly Murder* (1975), animals take revenge on humans for their acts of cruelty towards animals. Highsmith famously preferred the company of animals to that of people, keeping pet cats and even snails.

Highsmith seems not to have formed long-term close relationships. In 1960, she shared a farmhouse outside New Hope, Pennsylvania, with the lesbian author Marijana Meaker. In 1963, she moved to the south of England to be with her lover, the wife of a London businessman. After the relationship ended she moved to France in 1967 and bought a house in Samois-sur-Seine, where she lived with her friend Elizabeth Lyne. In 1982, she moved to Switzerland, first settling in Aurigeno and then in Tegna, where she lived an increasingly reclusive life in a house that she had built to her own design.

In 1990, Highsmith was honored by the French government when she was named Officier dans l'Ordre des Arts et des Lettres (Officer of the Order of Arts and Letters). In 1991, she was nominated for the Nobel Prize in literature. She died of cancer in a hospital in Locarno, Switzerland, on February 4, 1995.

Chapters 1-10

The Talented Mr. Ripley opens with the protagonist, Tom Ripley, walking along a street in New York and noticing that he is being followed. Tom fears that he is about to be arrested because he has been operating a scam involving the Internal Revenue Service.

The man following Tom introduces himself as Mr. Herbert Greenleaf, the father of Dickie Greenleaf, a wealthy young man whom Tom once accompanied to a party. Under the impression that Tom is a friend of Dickie's, Mr. Greenleaf explains that Dickie has been in Europe for two years. Mr. Greenleaf wants Dickie to come home because Mrs. Greenleaf has leukemia and may not live long, and because he wants him to take up his responsibilities in the family boatbuilding firm. Dickie prefers to stay in Mongibello, a village in Italy, sailing and painting. Mr. Greenleaf asks Tom to go to Europe at his expense and persuade Dickie to come home. Seeing a chance to escape his precarious existence in New York, Tom accepts.

Tom sails for Europe. He writes to his Aunt Dottie, who brought him up, telling her that he is leaving the country on business. Tom is relieved to have achieved independence from his aunt, who is in the habit of calling him and his late father "sissy."

He feels he has wasted his life. He had come to New York wanting to be an actor, but had been rebuffed. As a child, he had fantasized about stabbing Aunt Dottie with her brooch and running away.

Media Adaptations

- *Plein Soleil*, or *Purple Noon* in the United States, is a French-language film adaptation of *The Talented Mr. Ripley*, starring Alain Delon (1960). It was directed by René Clément, produced by Raymond Hakim and Robert Hakim, and distributed by Titanus Distribuzione Spa. The film was released as a DVD by Miramax in 1996.

- *The Talented Mr. Ripley*, adapted as a film by Anthony Minghella and starring Matt Damon, Gwyneth

Paltrow, and Jude Law, was produced by Mirage Enterprises/Paramount and distributed by Miramax/Paramount (1999). The film was released as a DVD by Paramount in 2000.

Tom arrives in Mongibello and finds Dickie on the beach with his friend Marge Sherwood. Dickie receives Tom without warmth. Tom broaches the subject of Mr. Greenleaf's wish for his son to return home. Dickie is dismissive. Neither Dickie nor Marge invites Tom to stay at their houses. Tom thinks that Marge is in love with Dickie but that Dickie is indifferent to her.

Tom watches Dickie and Marge go sailing in Dickie's boat as if he, Tom, did not exist. Tom is not surprised that Dickie does not want to give up his carefree life here. He badly wants to make Dickie like him, but Dickie treats Tom coldly until Tom tells him that Mr. Greenleaf employed Tom to go to Mongibello especially to persuade Dickie to go home. Dickie is amused, and warms to Tom. Tom tells Dickie that he has a talent for figures, can forge a signature, and can impersonate anyone. Tom does an impersonation, which Dickie enjoys, but Marge is unimpressed. Dickie shows Tom his paintings, which Tom knows are bad. Tom feels that Marge is in the way of his forming a bond with Dickie. Dickie invites Tom to stay at his house, and Tom moves in.

Tom and Dickie take a trip to Naples and Rome. As they are about to board the bus, Dickie recognizes an old friend, the American Freddie Miles. Dickie and Freddie arrange to meet at a ski resort called Cortina later that year. When Tom and Dickie return to Mongibello, Tom notes with satisfaction that Marge seems jealous of his closeness to Dickie.

Dickie is concerned that Marge is being pushed out. He leaves Tom to visit Marge. Tom follows Dickie to her house, where he sees them embracing. Tom runs back to Dickie's house in a hysterical state and throws Dickie's art tools around. He puts on one of Dickie's suits. Impersonating Dickie, he tells an imaginary Marge that he does not love her, and mimes strangling her. He accuses the imaginary Marge's corpse of "interfering between Tom and me —No, not that! But there *is* a bond between us!" Dickie enters and sees Tom dressed in his clothes. He angrily tells Tom that Marge thinks he (Tom) is homosexual, and that he (Dickie) wants to make clear that he himself is not. Tom insists that he is not, either. Tom asks Dickie if he is in love with Marge. Dickie says he is not, but he cares about her.

Chapters 11-20

Tom asks Dickie to accompany him to Paris as part of a drugs scheme operated by a local crook. To Tom's disappointment, Dickie says the plan is crazy and that Tom is under no obligation to do as he does. Tom realizes a terrible truth: he and Dickie are not friends, and neither do they know one another.

Tom receives a letter from Mr. Greenleaf terminating their agreement, as Tom has been unsuccessful with Dickie. Tom feels afraid and alone. Dickie declines to go to Paris with Tom. Also, Dickie and Marge have bought a refrigerator, which implies that Dickie plans to stay in Mongibello with Marge rather than going traveling with Tom.

Tom and Dickie go to San Remo. On the train, Dickie tells Tom that he wants to go to Cortina alone, with Marge. When they reach Cannes, they see two men sitting together. Dickie makes a contemptuous comment about homosexuals and looks at Tom with distaste. Tom is ashamed, remembering Aunt Dottie's taunts about sissies. Tom feels both hatred and affection for Dickie. He senses that Dickie has rejected his friendship. He has an impulse to kill him and works out a way to do it. He could become Dickie and steal his identity. He could keep an apartment in Rome or Paris and receive Dickie's allowance check every month. He resembles Dickie enough to use his passport.

At San Remo, Tom persuades Dickie to take out a boat. When they are far from land, Tom suggests a swim. As Dickie is taking off his trousers, Tom hits him over the head with an oar, in an act of premeditated murder. Tom steals Dickie's rings. He ties the anchor rope around Dickie's ankles and heaves the body, with the cement anchor to weigh it down, over the side of the boat. He loses his balance and falls into the water. He hauls himself back into the bloodstained boat. He fills the boat with stones and sinks it.

Thinking of his new life using Dickie's money, Tom is happier than he has ever been. On returning to Mongibello, he tells Marge that Dickie is staying in Rome and wants Tom to bring some of his belongings to Rome. He plans to ask a local man to act as agent for the sale of Dickie's house, boat, and furniture. Next day, Tom tells Marge he has had a letter saying that Dickie intends to stay in Rome indefinitely and will not go to Cortina. Marge feels shocked and hurt.

Back in Rome, Tom practices speaking in Dickie's voice. He forges Dickie's handwriting in a letter to Marge, telling her in his persona as Dickie that he wants to be alone. He adds that he is studying painting under a man called Di Massimo. In her reply, Marge expresses surprise that Dickie is staying in Rome, and advises him to get away from Tom, whom she dislikes.

Tom goes to Paris as Dickie. For the first time ever, he feels comfortable at a party. He feels reborn as a new person. After the party, he realizes that he has forgotten to tell Freddie that he was not going to his party at Cortina, which took place nearly a month ago. He picks up a letter from Marge to Dickie, in which she says that she is going back to the United States. She asks Dickie to go with her on the same boat. Tom does not reply, and the next letter she writes is resigned to the apparent truth that Dickie does not wish to see her. Later, she writes saying that Fausto, the Italian friend of Dickie's who taught Tom Italian in Mongibello, is coming to Rome and intends to visit Dickie.

In Rome, Tom rents an apartment, where he lives as Dickie. He feels poised and confident. Money begins to flow in from the sale of Dickie's furniture. Tom is alone, yet not lonely, and feels blameless and free.

Tom receives a surprise visit at his apartment from Freddie, who is wondering why Dickie did not come to Cortina. Tom tells him that Dickie has gone out to lunch and that he is leaving for Sicily soon. Tom sees Freddie staring at Dickie's silver identification bracelet on his wrist. He knows what Freddie is thinking: that Tom and Dickie are in a homosexual relationship, that they are living together in Dickie's apartment, and that Dickie is making Tom presents of his jewellery. As Freddie leaves, Tom overhears him talking with Signora Buffi, the landlady. She is telling Freddie that only Mr. Greenleaf lives upstairs and that he has not gone out today. Freddie comes back, and Tom realizes his cover is blown. Tom kills Freddie by hitting him over the head with an ashtray. He makes Freddie's death look like a robbery by stealing his wallet. He feels that Freddie's death was sad, but that he is a victim of his "own dirty mind."

Tom walks Freddie's body to his car in a way that looks like one drunk man supporting another. He drives to the Via Appia Antica, an ancient Roman road lined with tombs, and dumps the body. He leaves Freddie's car outside a nightclub with the keys in the ignition, throws his wallet in a sewer, and returns home. He wonders how Freddie found out where he lived, and concludes that someone must have followed him home and informed Freddie.

Tom receives a telephone call from Fausto for Dickie. Impersonating Dickie, Tom tells him he is leaving for Naples and arranges to see him at the railway station, though inwardly, he has no intention of meeting him.

The police find Freddie's body. They know that he visited "Signor Greenleaf" yesterday and arrive to question Tom, or Dickie, as they think he is. Tom confirms that Freddie visited him. He says that Freddie was drunk when he left, but not too drunk to drive. Tom checks into a hotel to avoid any of Dickie's friends who might call on him. The newspapers report that Freddie was last seen at Dickie's house, but do not say that Dickie is a suspect. The same day, the bloodstained boat in which Tom killed Dickie is found near San Remo. Tom is terrified. He knows that if the police check the hotel registers for missing Americans, the name Richard Greenleaf would stand out, and Tom is now living as Dickie. In that case, it would be Tom Ripley who would be assumed missing and murdered, and Dickie would be suspected of murder. He falls asleep and dreams that Dickie is alive, having swum to safety.

The police call on Tom, thinking he is Dickie. They say that Tom Ripley is missing, perhaps dead. Tom says he believes he went back to the United

States a month ago. The police are suspicious Because Dickie Greenleaf has twice been near the scene of a murder (of Freddie and, as they believe, Tom).

Marge arrives at Tom's hotel room, looking for Dickie. Tom knows he has to keep Tom Ripley's clothes and passport for such emergencies as Marge turning up, but also because Dickie is a murder suspect and he may have to revert to being Tom. Tom tells Marge that Dickie is out being questioned by the police. To get rid of her, Tom arranges to meet her in five minutes at Angelo's bar, though he has no intention of going there.

Tom goes to Palermo, Sicily. Marge thinks that Tom and Dickie are having a homosexual relationship and writes a farewell letter to Dickie rebuking him for acting the coward in not telling her honestly. The Palermo police call, looking for Tom Ripley. Tom tells them that Tom Ripley is in Rome.

In Palermo, Tom feels lonely and sad. He had imagined acquiring a new circle of friends and a better life as Dickie, but he realizes that he will always have to keep a distance from people in order to avoid being found out. He receives a letter from Dickie's trust company suggesting that the signature acknowledging receipt of his allowance is forged. The company wants him to confirm that it is his (Dickie's). Panic-stricken, Tom wonders if the company has been tipped off by the police as a result of their investigations, but he writes back confirming that the signature is his.

Chapters 21-30

Tom receives a threatening letter from the police ordering him to come to Rome to be questioned regarding Tom Ripley, who is still missing. Tom is frightened. He plans to get rid of Dickie's belongings. He reads a newspaper report saying that Dickie, a friend of the murdered Freddie, is missing after a Sicilian holiday.

Tom goes to Venice and, in his own persona, declares himself to the police as Tom Ripley. He feels that going back to being Tom is a great sadness. He tells the police that he last saw Dickie in Rome, before he went to Sicily. The police say that Dickie (actually Tom) was seen supporting a possibly dead Freddie beside Freddie's car, so they want to talk to Dickie. Tom says he does not know where he is. When they ask if Dickie and Freddie had quarreled, Tom says that Dickie did not go to Freddie's party in Cortina. The police suggest that they may have quarreled over Marge, and Tom encourages this belief. Dickie's apparent forgeries against himself and the murder of Freddie, combined with his disappearance, have made him a suspect. The police do not suspect Tom of anything, and dismiss him.

Tom, as himself, writes to Mr. Greenleaf and Marge saying that he thinks Dickie may have killed himself over the strain of being questioned for Freddie's murder. Marge thinks Dickie is merely hiding.

Tom now lives as Tom Ripley in a grand house

in Venice, surrounded by antique pieces of art and furniture. He forges Dickie's will, leaving his income and estate to Tom, and seals it in an envelope, on which he writes that it is not to be opened until June. He is invited to parties by high society people who are fascinated by his association with the missing Dickie.

Marge comes to stay with Tom at his house. She chats with Tom about Dickie's disappearance, without suspecting him. Marge says that Mr. Greenleaf is in Rome, trying to find Dickie. Tom tells Marge that he failed to meet her at Angelo's in Rome because a man came to interview him for a job immediately after she left.

Mr. Greenleaf visits Tom and Marge in Venice. He has engaged an American private detective to try to find Dickie.

Tom receives a letter from Bob Delancey saying that the police have questioned him about an income tax fraud in which the culprit had used his house as the address to collect his checks.

Marge finds Dickie's rings in a box in Tom's house. Tom claims that Dickie gave them to him in Rome, in case anything happened to him, and that he had then forgotten about them. Instantly, Tom realizes he may have to kill Marge. He plans to hit her over the head with the shoe he is holding, dump her body in the canal, and claim she fell in. But Tom does not need to kill her, as she believes Tom's story. She thinks the rings prove that Dickie killed himself or changed his identity. Marge is grief-stricken, as for the first time, she believes that Dickie must be dead. Mr. Greenleaf also accepts this.

The detective, Alvin McCarron, arrives to question Tom. Tom adds to his previous story about the rings, saying that Dickie told Tom not to say anything about them. McCarron appears to conclude that Dickie may be hiding out after killing Freddie, and gives up the case.

Peter Smith-Kingsley, an English friend of Dickie's who lives in Venice, invites Tom to stay at his house in Ireland. Tom declines, as Peter reminds him of Dickie and "the same thing that had happened with Dickie could happen with Peter." Close to tears, Tom wishes that he had done things differently with Dickie, so that he could have lived with him for the rest of his life.

Tom writes to Mr. Greenleaf in the United States, saying that he has opened an envelope that Dickie gave him marked "Not to be opened until June." He says it has turned out to be Dickie's will, in which he leaves his entire estate to Tom.

Tom plans to sail for Athens, Greece, imagining himself as an ancient Greek hero returning home. He hears that the police have found Dickie's paintings, signed with his name, and other belongings, at the American Express office in Venice. (Tom deposited them there under a false name after murdering Dickie, in case he should ever need them.) Tom worries that the police may find his fingerprints on the belongings.

Tom is nervous during his trip to Greece, fearing he will be arrested over the fingerprints and the forgery of the will. When Tom disembarks at the port of Piraeus, the police are waiting, but they are not looking for him. Tom reads a newspaper report that says that the fingerprints on Dickie's belongings are the same as those found in his (really Tom's) abandoned apartment in Rome. Therefore, the police assume that Dickie deposited the belongings himself and that he then committed suicide, was murdered, or is living under the false name given (actually by Tom) to the American Express office. At the Athens American Express office, Tom picks up a letter from Mr. Greenleaf, who has been convinced by the will that Tom forged that his son has committed suicide. He gives his blessing to Tom's inheriting Dickie's estate. Tom realizes ecstatically that Dickie's money and freedom are his. He tells a taxi driver to take him to the best hotel in town.

Characters

Dickie

Dickie (formally named Richard) Greenleaf is a wealthy young man who is the heir to his father's boatbuilding firm. While Mr. Greenleaf wants Dickie to join the family firm, Dickie asserts his independence by going to live in Mongibello, Italy, where he sails, paints, and collects his monthly allowance check courtesy of the family fortune. Dickie's family wealth allows him to live a carefree life of refined hedonism and to have fine things about him. It is this lifestyle that Tom covets and this is one of the factors that leads him to murder Dickie.

Dickie is a relative innocent who is too naïve to see Tom's true agenda in time to save himself. His good-heartedness is shown in his affection for Marge and his desire not to hurt her, though his self-absorption is shown in the fact that he is happy to spend time with her in the full knowledge that she is in love with him but that he cannot return her feelings. Dickie only likes Tom for a short period in the novel, quickly tiring of his dependence and becoming suspicious that Tom harbors homosexual feelings for him.

To some extent, Dickie shares Tom's tendency to pretend to be something he is not. His paintings are, as Tom recognizes, without merit, but he takes them seriously. However, Dickie's self-delusion, in contrast with Tom's, is harmless.

Dickie's conventional and non-criminal outlook on life provide a foil for Tom's character. For example, when Tom suggests that they go to Paris in a coffin as part of a drug smuggling scheme, Dickie thinks that the plan is "crazy." His judgment highlights Tom's unbalanced addiction to risk. As another example, Dickie's affectionate relationship with Marge contrasts with Tom's friendless existence.

Aunt Dottie

Aunt Dottie does not appear in person in the novel, but she is an influential force in Tom's life and character. After Tom's parents die, she brings him up in Boston. She remorselessly belittles him and his late father, saying that each is (or was, in the case of Tom's father) a "sissy," and repeatedly reminding Tom how much he costs her to bring up. Even as a child, Tom fantasizes about stabbing her with her brooch and running away, one of the first hints of his mental instability.

One of the reasons why Tom seizes the opportunity to go to Europe in Mr. Greenleaf's employ is to escape his dependence on Aunt Dottie, who is in the habit of sending him checks for small amounts of money, gestures that Tom views as insults.

Fausto

Fausto is a young Italian man who lives in Mongibello and who teaches Tom to speak Italian. He poses a danger to Tom when he decides to visit Dickie in Rome. Tom has murdered Dickie and is living in an apartment as Dickie, so he avoids meeting Fausto. Fausto is the Italian form of the German name Faust. In German legend, Faust sold his soul to the devil in return for worldly glory. It is symbolically significant that Tom receives Fausto's call immediately after he has murdered Freddie and dumped his body. The moment is a chilling reminder of how far into the depths of evil Tom has sunk.

Mr. Herbert Greenleaf

Mr. Greenleaf, Dickie's father, is the powerful and wealthy head of the Greenleaf family boatbuilding firm. He evidently cares for his son, but his autocratic nature demands that Dickie follow him into the family firm. Under the impression that Tom is a good friend of Dickie's, he employs Tom to go to Europe to bring back his stubborn son. Mr. Greenleaf's mistaken assumption about the closeness of the two younger men, along with his unfortunate choice of a compulsive liar, psychopath, and potential murderer for the task, testify to his obtuse instincts with regard to other people. Mr. Greenleaf is, however, shrewd enough to realize quickly that Tom is not going to succeed in his task. It is, perhaps, Mr. Greenleaf's blindness to the finer points of human relationships that makes it easy for Tom to convince him that Dickie has died or willfully disappeared and that Dickie bequeathed his entire estate to Tom.

Mrs. Greenleaf

Mrs. Greenleaf, Dickie's mother, only briefly appears in the novel. She has leukemia, and according to her husband, does not have long to live.

Richard Greenleaf

See Dickie

Alvin McCarron

Alvin McCarron is the private detective whom Mr.Greenleaf hires to look for the missing Dickie. Though not unintelligent, he is no match for Tom, who manipulates him into suspecting Dickie of murdering Freddie. He gives up the case and returns to the United States.

Freddie Miles

Freddie is an old friend of Dickie's from the United States. He encounters Dickie and Tom as they are leaving for their trip to Rome and Naples, and arranges with Dickie to meet him at a ski resort, Cortina, later in the year. When Dickie does not turn up at Cortina (because he is dead), Freddie's suspicions are aroused. His search for Dickie at what he believes to be his apartment in Rome leads to his finding out that Tom is not what he pretends to be, and Tom kills Freddie to protect his secret. Freddie's role in the plot is thus to provide suspense by almost managing to reveal Tom as a fraud, and to solidify Tom's reputation as a cold-blooded murderer.

Tom Ripley

Tom Ripley is the protagonist and hero of the novel, which is narrated in the third person but from his point of view. Orphaned at an early age, Tom was brought up in Boston by his Aunt Dottie.

Tom is an unusual hero in that he is an amoral young man who starts the novel as a minor conman and ends it as a double murderer. At the novel's beginning, he lies constantly about the most trivial details of his life in an effort to make himself appear more important than he is. For example, he tells Mr. Greenleaf that he works in advertising and was educated at Princeton, when in fact he has had a series of humble jobs and the closest he got to Princeton was to pump a Princeton student for information, foreseeing a time when the information might come in useful. Tom's talent for lying proves crucial to his success in getting away with two murders, as he frequently has to concoct false stories to throw his victims' friends and the police off the scent. He has little conscience and has the potential to become a serial killer, which, in fact, he becomes in subsequent Ripley novels. At the time Highsmith wrote *The Talented Mr. Ripley*, the heroes of most suspense and crime novels were morally upright and straight-talking detectives, policemen, or victims of crime who were trying to solve the crime and bring the criminal to justice. Tom, on the other hand, is a force for dishonesty, immorality, and destructiveness. He brings chaos in his wake, first disrupting and taking away the hitherto contented lives of Dickie and Freddie, and bringing grief to Marge and sorrow to Dickie's parents, one of whom is terminally ill.

It is a critical commonplace to call Tom charming, but there is little evidence for this quality when Tom is being himself. Charming people are easily liked, whereas many characters react to Tom with distaste, dislike, and mistrust. What is more, the better they get to know him, they less they like him. This is true of Dickie, Marge, Freddie, and even, after his initial optimism has worn off, Mr. Greenleaf. Tom is sensitive enough to be highly aware of the effect he has on others, and this knowledge tortures him. Before he assumes Dickie's identity, he writhes and squirms in social situations, acutely conscious of what he sees as his inferiority. He is, however, a consummate opportunist, and he has the skill, when under pressure, of manipulating people to do what he wants. For example, he risks being dismissed by Dickie in his first few days in Mongibello, and determines to make Dickie like him. He has the idea of telling Dickie that Mr. Greenleaf employed him specifically to bring Dickie home to the United States. This amuses

Dickie, who warms to Tom. This is not charm at work, but a desperate desire for approval and a calculated manipulation of others' emotions.

Similarly, Tom does not charm his way out of the many close scrapes he gets into with the police and Dickie's friends. Rather, he has the ability to impersonate sincerity and innocence, and the resourcefulness to think of a plausible answer to any probing question.

When Tom assumes Dickie's identity, he does acquire a charm that comes of being comfortable in his (or rather, Dickie's) skin for the first time in his life. He is confident and at ease at parties. Paradoxically, he is also lonely, because he dares not allow people to get to know him in case they discover his secret. Apart from his fear of getting caught, his positive motivations to keep up the pretence are first, because he enjoys having Dickie's money and influence, and second, because he thrives on the risk of being found out, and on the challenge of outwitting his pursuers every time with his ingenuity, talent, and luck.

Marge Sherwood

Marge is a young American woman who lives in Mongibello and who is in love with Dickie. She is an aspiring writer and appears to be more realistic about her talents than Dickie is about his—by the novel's end, she has a good chance of having her novel published.

Marge treats Dickie with loyalty and affection,

attempting to remain on friendly terms with him even when he has apparently cast her off (after Tom has murdered him). She is immediately suspicious of Tom when he arrives in Mongibello, marking her out as the most perceptive character in the novel. It is not possible to know how much of her suspicions center on her perception of Tom as a rival for the attention and affection of Dickie, and how much is an instinctive realization that Tom's motives are not pure. Probably, both factors are at work.

Marge acts as the antagonist to Tom in the first part of the novel, since, as he sees it, she stands in the way of his relationship with Dickie. Tom thinks of her with a certain contempt and even disgust, and cannot bear to see her underwear around his apartment when she comes to stay. Sneering at her enthusiasm, friendliness, and cheerfulness, he dismisses her as a "typical Girl Scout." However, these qualities, standing in stark contrast to the moroseness and cynicism of Tom, make her a sympathetic character. The fact that she finally believes Tom's account of events and accepts his claimed honest motives at face value is both a testament to her generous nature and to his skill at persuasion.

Peter Smith-Kingsley

Peter Smith-Kingsley is an English friend of Dickie's who lives in Venice. Tom declines Peter's invitation to his country house in Ireland as Peter reminds him of Dickie and "the same thing that had happened with Dickie could happen with Peter." Tom then breaks down in tears, believing that if he had managed things differently, he might have been able to live with Dickie for the rest of his life. Peter is therefore a catalyst character whose resemblance to Dickie brings out the closest approximation to love, and a crisis of conscience, that Tom ever feels.

Subversion of Conventional Morality

The Talented Mr. Ripley subverts conventional morality in several ways. First, the hero is a criminal. This contrasts with most literary heroes, who are fundamentally admirable, however flawed they may be. In particular, novels about crime often feature a hero who is morally upright and honest, who is trying to solve the crime and bring the criminal to justice.

Highsmith rejected these conventions with her criminal hero Tom Ripley, who not only gets away with murder, but is rewarded with the wealth of his victim, Dickie Greenleaf. This is partly an assertion by Highsmith of realism over the conventions of crime fiction. Highsmith said in a 1981 interview with Diana Cooper-Clark in *Armchair Detective*, "that only 11 percent of murders are solved."

Tom is even able to add happiness to the list of spoils he gains from murdering Dickie, contrary to the literary convention that the murderer is tortured by his deed until he receives his just deserts. After he kills Dickie, Tom has an "ecstatic moment", falling asleep "happy, content, and utterly confident, as he had never been before in his life." He feels happier impersonating Dickie than he did as himself, a sort of moral irony that gains its power from the reader's familiarity with the convention that people who live a lie must be unhappy.

Highsmith encourages her readers to collude in moral subversion by sympathizing with Tom, the criminal. While readers may not find Tom likable, he is more interesting than the conventionally virtuous characters, such as the Greenleafs, Marge, and Freddie. In addition, Highsmith's sensitive examination of Tom's outsider status may encourage readers to sympathize with him on the emotional level even while they disapprove of or dislike him on the moral and intellectual levels. Consequently, readers may be pleased to see him walk free at the novel's end, thereby supporting the moral subversion that underlies the novel.

Reality and Unreality

The novel is narrated from Tom's point of view, and Tom has an elastic concept of the truth. To Tom, there is an atmosphere of unreality about New York, as if the city "was putting on a show just for him." Even before he arrives in Mongibello, he lies about many aspects of his life, generally with the aim of making himself appear more successful than he is, and also to protect himself. He tells Mr. Greenleaf he works in advertising, and constructs a fictional story about going to Princeton. An element of premeditation went into the latter lie: Tom pumped a Princeton student for information about his life because he felt it might come in useful one day. The only truth he tells Mr. Greenleaf is that he was brought up by his Aunt Dottie. Aunt Dottie's humiliations are a formative influence that Tom recalls just before he murders Dickie. Aunt Dottie represents the terrible truth about Tom's life, that he feels inferior and despised. Her taunt, "*Sissy! He's a sissy from the ground up. Just like his father!*" is the jumping-off point for Tom's life of crime and deception.

From the point when Tom murders Dickie, he begins to live the lies that he formerly told. He used to lie about being successful; now that he has taken on Dickie's identity, he is indeed successful, wealthy, and socially respected. Moreover, he comes actually to believe his own lies: "His stories were good because he imagined them intensely, so intensely that he came to believe them." Perhaps this is why others are convinced by his lies. Time and again after the murders, and frequently with the odds stacked against him, Tom is able to convince his victims' friends, and the police, that his fictional version of events is both plausible and correct. In this respect, he resembles an artist or writer who creates an act of the imagination and persuades people that it is the truth. There is an implied comparison between Marge, the conventional writer, whose achievement in getting interest from a publisher is modest, and Tom, who effectively writes his own new life and has it accepted as fact, and in the process gains a fortune and an impressive new persona.

Topics for Further Study

- Consider some of the names of people or places that Highsmith uses in *The Talented Mr. Ripley.* Examples include Thomas Ripley, Dickie Greenleaf, Marge Sherwood, *Pipistrello* (the name of Dickie's boat), Otello's (a restaurant), and Fausto. What contribution to the story or characters do these names make by means of their associations? The first three examples require you only to think about simple word associations; the last three may require some research. Write a short paragraph on each name.

- Watch Anthony Minghella's movie version of *The Talented Mr. Ripley.*

How accurate a depiction of the novel is it? What changes have been made, and what effect do they have on the characters, plot, moral tone, and the sympathies of the audience? Write an essay on your findings.

- Research the psychological definition of the term *psychopath*. To what extent does Tom Ripley fit this type? Give a class presentation on your findings using concrete examples from the novel.

- Research social attitudes toward homosexuality in the 1950s and compare them to social attitudes today. How have they changed, how have they stayed the same? Gather as much information as you can before presenting your findings to the class.

- Write a short story or screenplay about a murder from the point of view of either the murderer, or a person who is trying to solve the crime. Write a separate essay on how the point of view affects your plot, characters, moral tone and stance, and how it might affect the sympathies of your readers or audience.

The theme of reality and unreality extends to emphasize the malleable nature of identity. During the course of the novel, Tom lives first as himself, then steals Dickie's identity and lives as Dickie, and finally resumes his own identity, but with Dickie's wealth. These transformations are largely based on his manipulation of the means by which society defines identity: passports, handwriting, signatures, and wills. Such means are exposed by the events of the novel as superficial, fragile, and ultimately, unreal.

Homosexuality and Society

Homosexuality and society's attitudes to it are a constant underlying subtext in the novel. The theme is introduced in the first pages, with Tom wondering whether his pursuer is a "pervert." This was a common word in the 1950s for a homosexual, and its derogatory nature indicates the level of disapproval leveled against homosexuals by society in general.

In spite of Tom's apparent anxiety about homosexuals, his own feelings for Dickie have homoerotic undertones. In chapter 10, Tom sees Dickie embracing Marge and throws a violent tantrum. He throws Dickie's art tools around and removes Dickie's suit from the closet. It is possible that Highsmith introduced this incident in a tongue-in-cheek fashion to refer to Tom's feelings for Dickie, as the word *closet* meaning *secret* began to be applied to homosexuals in the mid-twentieth century. In removing Dickie's suit from the closet, is Tom figuratively enticing him into a homosexual relationship with himself, one that he assumes will be more rewarding than Dickie's relationship with Marge? In a chilling episode that prefigures events to come, Tom puts on Dickie's suit and, impersonating him, tells an imaginary Marge that he does not love her. Then he kills the imaginary Marge, accusing her of "interfering between Tom and me—No, not that! But there *is* a bond between us!"

Tom is denying any homosexual feelings for Dickie, but his denial is not convincing. He does not express or act on any homosexual feelings, but with good reason, as both Dickie and his friend Freddie express contempt and disgust for homosexual behavior. The shame that Tom feels at his sexuality is revealed in the incident that prompts him to murder Dickie. They see some men who may be homosexuals on a beach, and Dickie voices his contempt towards them, then looks at Tom with distaste, as if he is also homosexual. The episode recalls to Tom's mind Aunt Dottie's taunting of him as a sissy (an effeminate person). The homoerotic theme continues when Dickie's final act, before Tom murders him, is to remove his trousers.

Tom comes closest to admitting the nature of his feelings for Dickie long after Dickie is dead. Reminded of Dickie by his friend Peter Smith-Kingsley, Tom gives way to genuine tears, reflecting that if he had done things differently, "he *could* have lived with Dickie for the rest of his life."

This, like much of what Tom says and does, is a lie or self-delusion, as Dickie appears not to care about Tom.

Dickie and Freddie reflect the antagonistic attitude of 1950s society to homosexuality. While Tom does fall into the crime novel stereotype of the sinister homosexual who kills the object of his or her thwarted affections, he also expresses the more liberal and humane view: "Maybe Cannes was full of fairies. So what?"

Suspense Novel

Suspense novels, sometimes called psychological suspense novels, are usually, though not always, crime or detective novels that have a misdeed at their center. They differ from crime or detective novels, however, in that they do not address the question of who did the crime. Suspense novels focus on the threat of violent physical action and danger, or the danger and action itself, while also offering lively entertainment.

All novels use suspense as a device to make the reader continue reading. The suspense question may be *Will the boy get the girl?* or *Will she succeed in becoming a Broadway star?*. In *The Talented Mr. Ripley*, the suspense question of the first part of the book is how the uneasy triangle between Tom, Dickie, and Marge will be worked out. The question changes after Dickie's murder to whether Tom will get away with it.

The difference between ordinary fiction containing suspense and a suspense novel lies in the way in which the suspense question is answered. A suspense novel seeks to engage the reader's intellect and emotions. The intellectual part of the answer lies in the detail of how the criminal perpetrates his crime, or how the detective solves it. The emotional part of the answer lies in the trajectory of the passions that led up to the crime, and the emotional consequences of the crime. It is noteworthy that in *The Talented Mr. Ripley*, Highsmith keeps up the suspense to the last page.

Irony

The Talented Mr. Ripley is a novel laden with irony of the type that arises from a discordance between acts and results. There is a perceived gap between an understanding or expectation of reality, and what actually happens. The fact that Tom feels so comfortable in his stolen identity as Dickie is ironic, as it might be expected that he would feel less comfortable when living a lie. There is also heavy irony in the fact that at the end of the novel, Tom expects to be arrested as a result of the fingerprints the police took from the belongings of Dickie that Tom deposited at the American Express office, whereas the fingerprints actually convince the police he is innocent. This is because the fingerprints on the belongings are the same as those found in the apartment in Rome that the police believe Dickie lived in, though in fact, Tom lived there disguised as Dickie.

Dramatic irony occurs when the reader or audience knows something that the character does not, adding a new level of meaning to the character's action or words of which the character is ignorant. An example is when Marge writes to Dickie (in fact, Tom masquerading as Dickie) that she has told the police "that you and Tom are inseparable and how they could have found you and still missed *Tom*, I could not imagine." Unknown to Marge, Tom and Dickie are literally inseparable, as they are one and the same person.

The effect of such irony in the novel is two-fold. First, it underlines Highsmith's purpose of moral subversion, in that morally wrong actions end up being rewarded. Second, it establishes a distance between the narrator and the events and characters, as if the narrator is viewing them with a certain wry humor.

Juxtaposition of the Macabre and the Banal

In the novel, macabre episodes such as Tom's murders of Dickie and Freddie are described in plain, everyday, non-descriptive prose, as if the events were no more remarkable than someone going to buy a carton of milk. The effect of this is to remind readers that the line between a psychopath like Tom and the rest of humanity is a fine one. It also shows readers that seemingly ordinary people such as Tom can be concealing shocking pathology. This is evident in scenes like the one in which Dickie catches Tom impersonating him in his suit, yet Tom is able to quickly resume an appearance of rationality.

Menace

Highsmith builds an atmosphere of menace

leading up to Tom's murdering Dickie in two main ways. First, she shows evidence of Tom's mental pathology, which increases in seriousness as the novel progresses. He is shown fantasizing about murdering Aunt Dottie from eight years old, lying, and breaking the law. When his fascination with Dickie's lifestyle renders him part of a triangle of tension between him, Dickie, and Marge, it is obvious that at least one of these characters will suffer. The threat of Tom's unstable personality reaches its height in the scene in which Tom puts on Dickie's suit, impersonates him, and mimes murdering Marge on the grounds that she was "interfering between Tom and me." It is clear to the reader that something terrible is going to happen, but Dickie is too naïve to view the threat as seriously as he should.

Setting as Metaphor

Highsmith uses the European setting of *The Talented Mr. Ripley* in a similar way to the American author Henry James in his book *The Ambassadors.* There is an implicit contrast between the innocence of the United States and the experience and corruption of the old European society. Europe is presented as a place where conventional morals and duties can be disregarded, and new roles taken on without accountability. It is significant that before Tom leaves the United States for Europe, Mr. Greenleaf asks him if he has read James' book.

Development of the Crime Novel

As well as belonging to the literary genre of the suspense novel, much of Highsmith's work, including *The Talented Mr. Ripley*, also belongs to the wider category of the crime novel. The rise of the crime novel as a genre occurred in late nineteenth-and early twentieth-century England, with the appearance of Sir Arthur Conan Doyle's Sherlock Holmes mysteries. From this time until Highsmith's *The Talented Mr. Ripley* appeared, most crime novels featured an honest hero who brought the criminal to justice. This is particularly true of mainstream crime fiction written between World Wars I and II (1918-1939), which leaves no room for doubt that virtue lies with the forces of law and order and evil lies with the criminal, who ends up being punished.

Compare & Contrast

- **1950s:** In the United States, sexual acts between men are illegal in most states under sodomy laws. Homosexuals are stigmatized as being abnormal, diseased, or threats to national security.

  Today: While stigmatization

continues in some regions, anti-homosexual laws are repealed or invalidated. In 2007, a bill outlawing discrimination against employees because of sexual orientation is introduced into Congress.

- **1950s:** Highsmith rejects the conventions of mainstream crime fiction by portraying the hero of *The Talented Mr. Ripley* as a criminal who gets away with murder.
  Today: Fictional figures such as the criminal hero and the morally compromised policeman or detective, have become common in crime fiction, drama, and films. However, it is still unusual to find criminal heroes who are not punished in any way for their crimes.

- **1950s:** Fingerprinting is one of the few scientific means of identifying criminals available to the police. In *The Talented Mr. Ripley*, however, fingerprinting works in Tom's favor to clear him of a crime he really did commit.
  Today: DNA profiling, whereby genetic material in tissue residues found at a crime scene is analyzed to provide identification of an individual, is widely used in crime

solving. If DNA profiling had been available to the police in *The Talented Mr. Ripley*, Tom would likely have been convicted.

During the 1920s and 1930s, a new type of morally compromised hero emerged with the appearance of a genre known as hardboiled crime fiction. Pioneered by writers such as Dashiell Hammett in the late 1920s and Raymond Chandler from the late 1930s, this genre featured detective heroes who were not averse to using violence and underhanded methods in solving crimes. Out of the hardboiled genre emerged a subgenre known as noir fiction. In noir fiction, the protagonist is usually not a detective, but a victim, suspect, or perpetrator of crime. Other features are that sexual relationships are used to advance the plot and the lead characters have self-destructive qualities. The American writer James M. Cain is considered to be one of the founders of noir fiction, with his novel *The Postman Always Rings Twice* (1934). Beginning in the 1940s, noir tendencies found their way into Hollywood crime dramas, creating the genre known as *film noir*.

Highsmith's novel *The Talented Mr. Ripley* built on these trends to present a criminal hero who gets away with his crimes and appears not to suffer as a result. In her portrayal of Tom Ripley, Highsmith was able to draw upon the growing field of psychology to examine the roots and nature of his malaise. From the 1950s, crime and suspense novels contained a substantial complement of psychological insight and analysis. This is one of the factors that enabled Highsmith and other writers to thrust the criminal protagonist to center stage.

The Psychopath

Tom Ripley is frequently discussed in critical works as a type of mentally ill person known as a psychopath. Individuals who might now be classed as psychopaths were first described by the Frenchman Philippe Pinel (1745-1826), who is widely considered to be the father of modern psychiatry. He described patients who were insane in the sense that they seemed rational but lacked restraint and remorse for their harmful actions.

The next most influential work on psychopathy was carried out by the American psychiatrist Hervey Cleckley. In his book, *The Mask of Sanity* (1941), Cleckley lists the characteristics of the psychopath, including superficial charm and good intelligence, lack of remorse or shame, inadequately motivated social behavior, poor judgment and failure to learn by experience, unreliability, pathologic egocentricity and inability to love.

Although the term *psychopathy* is in widespread use, it is not listed as a mental condition in the *Diagnostic and Statistical Manual of Mental Disorders* published by the American Psychiatric Association, a handbook for mental health professionals that lists mental disorders and the criteria for diagnosing them. The closest correlate to psychopathy listed is antisocial personality disorder (ASPD), and the two terms are frequently used interchangeably by psychiatrists, many of whom consider that psychopathy differs from ASPD only in respect of its severity. This equation between ASPD and psychopathy is, however, disputed by some authorities, including a leading expert in the field, Robert D. Hare. Most psychopaths meet the criteria for ASPD, but not all people with ASPD are psychopaths. According to the *Diagnostic and Statistical Manual of Mental Disorders*, ASPD is characterized by the individual's lack of empathy, disregard for the rights and feelings of others, superficial charm, inflated self-appraisal, deceitfulness and manipulation for his or her own ends, disregard for social and legal rules, irresponsibility, aggression, and sudden changes of jobs, residences, or relationships.

ASPD is called dissocial personality disorder by the World Health Organization. In its publication, *The ICD-10 Classification of Mental and Behavioural Disorders*, it lists the criteria for diagnosis of dissocial personality disorder as follows, stipulating that at least three of these criteria must be met:

- Callous unconcern for the feelings of others
- Gross and persistent attitude of irresponsibility and disregard for social norms, rules, and obligations
- Incapacity to maintain enduring

relationships, though having no difficulty in establishing them

- Very low tolerance to frustration and a low threshold for discharge of aggression, including violence

- Incapacity to experience guilt or to profit from experience, particularly punishment

- Marked proneness to blame others, or to offer plausible rationalizations, for the behavior that has brought the patient into conflict with society

Attitudes about Homosexuality

In the United States and much of Europe in the 1950s, homosexuality was taboo. Homosexual men, in particular, could lose their jobs and official positions if their sexual orientation was revealed. Many politicians treated homosexuality as a sign of anti-American attitudes, marking out the homosexual as a threat to national security. This connection was also made by the Nazis during World War II, who exterminated homosexuals alongside Jews, gypsies, mentally and physically disabled people, and other minorities in the Holocaust. In the United States from the late 1940s to the late 1950s, Senator Joseph McCarthy used accusations of homosexuality as a smear tactic in his anti-communist crusade, combining the Red Scare against supposed communists with the so-called Lavender Scare against homosexuals.

Homosexuality has long been seen by some segments of the population as a disease or disorder. Only as late as 1973 did the American Psychiatric Association vote to remove homosexuality from its *Diagnostic and Statistical Manual of Mental Disorders*. Some groups, particularly certain Christian groups, believe that homosexuality is a mental disease that can be cured by means of psychological conditioning programs.

Since the late twentieth century, a growth in the field of genetics has prompted the search for a homosexuality gene. This has raised fears among some homosexual rights groups that the purpose of such research is to modify or eliminate these genes (if any such genes exist).

As of 2007, many countries maintain laws that prohibit or regulate sexual activity between consenting adults of the same sex. In the United States, state sodomy laws, which made sexual acts between homosexual men illegal, were repealed in most states during the last half of the twentieth century, from the 1960s onwards. The remaining anti-homosexual laws were invalidated by the 2003 Supreme Court decision *Lawrence et al. v. Texas*, in which the court struck down the prohibition of homosexual sodomy in Texas. On April 24, 2007, the Employment Non-Discrimination Act, was first proposed in Congress. This potential federal law would disallow discrimination based on gender identity or sexual orientation in the United States.

Critical Overview

Highsmith's work was largely ignored in the United States during her lifetime. Possible reasons for this include her less-than-friendly personality and reputation for misanthropy (a dislike or distrust of all humankind). She was also unpopular for her public criticism of twentieth-century U.S. foreign policy. She did, however, enjoy great popularity in the United Kingdom, France, Spain, Germany, Switzerland, and Austria. Typical of the unenthusiastic critical response to her work in the United States at this time is a remark by Anthony Boucher in a 1956 *New York Times Book Review* article. Commenting on Highsmith's receipt of the Edgar Allan Poe Scroll of the Mystery Writers of America award for *The Talented Mr. Ripley*, Boucher concedes that the novel is "good," but adds that it is "hard to envision in the year's best class."

Since Highsmith's death in 1995, however, her reputation has risen in the United States. Her Ripley novels were republished, and her increasing popularity was solidified by Anthony Minghella's 1999 film version of *The Talented Mr. Ripley*. One factor that may have contributed to the change in her reputation in the United States is the growing tendency to view society as an uncertain milieu in which evil is not always punished and good does not always prosper, a viewpoint that prevails in Highsmith's novels. Another factor is her sympathetic portrayal of homosexual and lesbian relationships, which has earned her an important place in gay and lesbian literature.

In the wake of Mingella's film, a new, and very different, range of reviews of the republished Ripley novels appeared. Writing in the *San Francisco Chronicle*, Oscar C. Villalon praises Highsmith as "one of the finest American writers of crime fiction." He adds, "she raised herself above genre with her unsettling view of who we are and how killing can be as unremorseful and easy as breathing."

In a review of the Everyman anthology, *The Talented Mr. Ripley, Ripley Under Ground, Ripley's Game* for the *New York Times*, Michiko Kakutani notes Highsmith's ability to create a "chilly, misanthropic world." This is a world, explains Kakutani, in which "murderers are rarely caught, much less brought to justice; a world in which identity is permeable and the macabre and the banal, the insane and the rational, live serenely side by side."

In Europe, Highsmith's popularity continues to grow. In 2000, the London *Times* named *The Talented Mr. Ripley* as one of its "100 Best Crime Novels of the 20th Century." The anonymous reviewer remarks on the charisma of the novel's protagonist, noting that "Tom Ripley is the sort of double murderer it's hard not to take a shine to," and adding: "you want him to get away with it—and he does." In her article for the London *Times*, Zoe Paxton draws attention to Highsmith's ability "to show the world through the eyes of her most despicable characters." Paxton points out that these people are not outside humanity: "They are everyday people doing unspeakable things in such an everyday way that you start, bit by bit, to realise that it could be you." The details are so banal, Paxton notes, and the prose so neutral and direct, that the reader begins to identify with the person. This, says Paxton, is why Highsmith's stories are so haunting: "you realise that there is no way of escaping what humans are."

What Do I Read Next?

- The next novel in Highsmith's Ripley series after *The Talented Mr. Ripley* is *Ripley Under Ground* (1970). The novel shows Tom married and living a life of luxury in France. He collects art and sells fake paintings to supplement his income.

- *Mystery and Suspense Writers: The*

Literature of Crime, Detection, and Espionage, edited by Robin W. Winks and Maureen Corrigan (1998), is a two-volume collection of over eighty articles on mystery, detective, and espionage fiction. The editors include biographies and criticism of writers such as Edgar Allen Poe, Patricia Highsmith, and Sarah Paretsky. There are also essays on subgenres such as the police procedural, the spy novel, and the whodunit.

- *The Postman Always Rings Twice* (1934), by James M. Cain, is a pioneering noir novel that set a precedent (or example) for the entire genre. It tells the story of a drifter who falls in love with the wife of the owner of a rural diner. The two begin a secret affair and plot to kill the woman's husband. The novel is a bleak, moody, and oddly compelling read.

- Highsmith once told an interviewer that the only suspense writing she read was by the Russian author Fyodor Dostoevsky. In her book *Plotting and Writing Suspense Fiction*, she wrote, "I think most of Dostoyevsky's books would be called suspense books, were they being published today for the first time." Dostoevksy's novel *The Brothers Karamazov* (1880) is a classic and prototypical suspense novel.

- Robert J. Corber's book *Homosexuality in Cold War America: Resistance and the Crisis of Masculinity* (1997) examines how homosexual men in the 1950s resisted pressure to remain in the closet. Corber argues that a gay male identity emerged in the 1950s that both drew on and transcended left-wing opposition to the cultural and political consensus of the Cold War. He explores novels, plays, and films of the period as well as social trends such as the national security state, the growth of the suburbs, and consumer culture to develop his ideas.

Sources

Boucher, Anthony, "Criminals at Large," in the *New York Times Book Review*, May 6, 1956, p. 303.

Cleckley, Hervey, M.D., *The Mask of Sanity: An Attempt to Clarify Some Issues about the So-Called Psychopathic Personality*, Emily S. Cleckley, 1941, 5th edition, 1988, pp. 338-39.

Diagnostic and Statistical Manual of Mental Disorders DSM-IV-TR, American Psychiatric Association, 2000, pp. 701-03.

Greene, Graham, Foreword, in *Eleven*, by Patricia Highsmith, Atlantic Monthly Press, 1989, p. x.

Highsmith, Patricia, *Plotting and Writing Suspense Fiction*, St. Martin's Griffin, 1983.

———, *The Talented Mr. Ripley*, Vintage, 1999.

Highsmith, Patricia, and Diana Cooper-Clark, "An Interview with Patricia Highsmith," in *Armchair Detective*, Vol. 14, No. 4, Spring 1981, pp. 313-20.

The ICD-10 Classification of Mental and Behavioural Disorders: Clinical Descriptions and Diagnostic Guidelines, World Health Organization, 1993, p. 159.

Kakutani, Michiko, "Books of the Times: The Kinship of Macabre and Banal," in the *New York Times*, November 19, 1999.

King James Bible, Romans 6:23, Galatians 6:7,

http://quod.lib.umich.edu/k/kjv (accessed July 30, 2007).

Lawrence et al. v. Texas, 539 U.S. 558 (2003), http://www.law.cornell.edu/supct/html/02-102.ZS.html (accessed July 30, 2007).

"100 Best Crime Novels of the 20th Century," in the *Times*, September 30, 2000, p. 4.

Paxton, Zoe, "Mistress of the Banality of Evil," in the *Times*, October 8, 2005, p. 15.

Villalon, Oscar C., "The Talented Ms. Highsmith: 'Ripley' Author Transcended Crime Genre with Unsettling Insights into Evil," in the *San Francisco Chronicle*, January 11, 2000, p. B-1.

Further Reading

Hare, Robert D., *Without Conscience: The Disturbing World of the Psychopaths among Us*, Guilford Press, 1999.

> Hare argues in this book that psychopaths are aware of the difference between right and wrong but ignore the distinction. In addition, they are egocentric and have no feelings of empathy, guilt, or remorse. While Hare draws on scientific research, he presents the material in a way that is accessible to the layperson.

Harrison, Russell, *Patricia Highsmith*, Twayne's United States Author Series, Twayne Publishers, 1997.

> Aimed at anyone from advanced high school students to university professors, this book is a critical introduction to the author and her work, setting it in the context of major literary trends.

Mawer, Noel, *Critical Study of the Fiction of Patricia Highsmith: From the Psychological to the Political*, Edwin Mellen Press, 2004.

> This book presents a thorough critical analysis of Highsmith's work.

Mawer goes beyond the discussion of the author's suspense writing to explore her intense character studies.

Wilson, Andrew, *Beautiful Shadow: A Life of Patricia Highsmith*, Bloomsbury, 2003.

This candid biography of Highsmith draws upon her journals, letters, and exclusive interviews with friends and associates. Wilson reveals her intelligence and frankness but does not attempt to gloss over the characteristics about her that others have criticized, including racial prejudice, anti-Semitism, cruelty, and insensitivity.

Printed in October 2023
by Rotomail Italia S.p.A., Vignate (MI) - Italy